Singing Lessons

Also by Kevin McIlvoy

A Waltz
The Fifth Station
Little Peg
Hyssop
The Complete History of New Mexico
57 Octaves Below Middle C
At the Gate of All Wonder
One Kind Favor
Is It So? Glimpses, Glyphs, & Found Novels

Singing Lessons

POEMS

Kevin McIlvoy

Press 53
Winston-Salem

Press 53, LLC
PO Box 30314
Winston-Salem, NC 27130

First Edition

Library of Congress Control Number
2024931881

ISBN 978-1-950413-77-5

In joy

Contents

Introduction   xi

I

The River Scratch

Rose—Blessed Art   5
Zaum   6
Portage   9
I would give, I tell you   13
Comparable miracles   14
Awake, thinking himself asleep,   16
Love poem   17
Estivation   18
Mrs. Passerat transmits the gospel, 1968   20
Troubled guest   21
Nap   22
Tilt-up   23
What I've got so far is   24
An afternoon in Troup County, Georgia   26
Another miracle in the life of Sam Sierra   28
Ladder   31
He cast upstream again, mended   33

What a Dancer Does

Thanksgiving   37
You are my feed.   38
The Bronze Level   39
Interrupting Issa's nap, sparrows sing and call—
    an old man amidst them says,   40
Click & drag to look around   41
Radicle   43
Mrs. P: a lesson on warming the voice   44
The Man Rose   45

Seating chart   48
Play "White Rabbit"! Play "White Rabbit"!   50
Prose poem by God   51
Gemels   52
A golden ratio day   54

II

The daylight waltz   57

III

The River Scratch

Selfie   69
Oh, that.   71
Tribute   72
At 70   75
Cairn   77
If it's clear where you are   79
Why Owen Park   80
Mrs. P: the practice of creaky voice   81
Stacey Abrams returns to Troup County, Georgia   82
12 doorways   85
Descriptions of Heaven   86
Rose   88
Once, walking   89
Sycamore   94
Finches   95

What a Dancer Does

The parable of the table   99
The fit of some thing against somethings   101
Privacy curtain   103
Mr. Shadowgee's blues   105
Solstice, December 21, 2019   106
Prayer in response to your fearful thoughts
    regarding critical race theory   108
Mrs. P, 1962: A singing lesson on arpeggio and glissando   109
Ore   110
Ultima Multis   112
—there one lies at ease   114
I am not a robot.   115
Cardiological   117
Kiln   119

Afterword   123
Acknowledgments   125
Notes   127
Author Biography   131

Introduction
by Brooks Haxton

When Mc played blues harp, he celebrated the essence of soulful improvisation. The language in his poems, as in his prose, is soulful music too.

When he read aloud, he made reading a musical improvisation, not by taking liberties with the writing, but in the sense that any virtuoso performance is improvisation, even when it delivers the soul of a composition precisely as it appears on the page. In spoken delivery, Mc used pitch, attack, pacing, and volume, the whole range of musical dynamics.

I heard him read dozens of times, poems and prose. He was one of my favorite readers. The variety of effects in his reading was not something he was adding to the words, but the delivery of an essence in the writing itself.

Mc was a first-rate musician of language before he learned blues harp. He had devoted himself for years to the study of spoken dynamics. He recorded various regional speech, people whose speech he found distinctive. He loved speech as a revelation of the one who speaks. Voices matter to his poems, as to his prose, as intimate contact with family, neighbors, friends, acquaintances, even with public figures. Poetic devices and received forms, like the ones we find in this collection, came to him as celebrations of delivery as well, which is to say as intensities of being human. His poems are the physical presence of the world delivered in the physical action of the voice.

Spoken idiom itself is an engine in a poem like "Tilt-up," where the speaker is a carpenter hurt by a crazed fellow worker with a nail-gun. He delivers his own story of bizarre personal injury, letting the event melt into his thoughts about various matters, including workers at various jobs and people in the ER working on him. The poem pays attention, like much of Mc's writing, to the mind of a person telling a story. It values attention to the world. Deeply sustained attentiveness is the essence of Mc's work, in this poem and everywhere.

In another poem, we note precise details of a natural scene, "one brown trout / sipping black ants fallen." The angler observing this also puts attention on the "entire love story" carved into an aspen beside the stream: "Q&K4ever—not." Fluidity and inclusiveness are hallmarks here.

Like many writers, Mc gravitated to projects that drew him into the delight of study. He spent years in the study of dance, and of singing, and drawing, which he pursued as profound pleasures in themselves, and shared in his writing as presences revealed in language. We value Mc's poems because their essence is an essence of poetry, a renewal of the world we celebrate in the joy of revelation.

I

The River Scratch

Often he reckons, in the dawn, them up.
Nobody is ever missing.

John Berryman, "Dream Song 29"

Rose—Blessed Art

she among women—would not permit me to say "goddamn"—she said, "B Francis, people who talk that way go to hell for a longer stay," something she learned from Mother Church so she told me over sixty years ago between rosaries meant to redeem me—If I wanted to push my luck I would say, Bobdammit!—or—I'll be Bobdamned! which made her laugh (bitterly) since it confirmed we had nothing we could agree upon, nothing unholy upon which we couldn't agree—my father who said "Goddamn!" whenever he pleased was later than my mother in becoming a poem, but after illness, brief wellness and terribler illness, he did became one, by which I mean a man who found his tune his time his riddling form—

Zaum

B. Francis, at seventy, has been balding
ever since his fontanel would not close
on time. He had worn gauze
beanies red as Lincoln roses
to kindergarten and to first
grade. His supermagic wristlet
explained his seizure powers
to the teachers and the school nurses,
to the nuns and the parish priests,
to the newest specialists and technicians.
To anyone who asked—always
plenty of those—he made a fist
and raised his chin and his chest,
and showed them the ID chain.

Until the age of nine, he applied medicine
that his mother, inextinguishable votive
candle, called Black Zaum Salve.
The container, same as a shoe polish can,
came open with a turn-pin. An
applicator inside, a guitar pick, was
his father's from his days as a rock musician.
The Black Zaum, a wax solution
stinking of turpentine, softened B's
scalp, made him known in any room
he entered. In sunlight it seeped, framed
his face almost to his jawline.
His father, a steel mill foreman,
brought him a hardhat of his own,
another costume element B had to explain.

The seizures increased in number and in
force. In a daily hatching effort, his egg-tooth brain
chipped at, scrawled the crust of his skull. His mother,
thinning, limp clothesline sheet, eyes and hair ashen,
returned to her silent realm, her sanitorium dorm,
to her required exercise regimens
on the steeply pitched cold porch.

The Ward, Nurse Arn called the place;
The Terminal, she named his mother's wing;
The Lot, the space for lounging; *The Moon*,
the site for examination, down a shining,
reflective long hall that lengthened when
the ceiling lights flickered or the Moon
door swung open.

On the morning she came home again
for his ninth birthday, B. Francis flung
his hat aside and with a hooked salmon's speed he ran
toward her, the tin edge of the half-opened
garage door shearing off the top of his scalp.

The muddy glop dropped at her feet. Blood pouring
from his unconcluded head, he held her,
heard her say, "Holy God," as she pressed her hand
down and passed him to his father who tucked him
like a football under his arm the whole reeling
drive, sitting him up only at the hospital, compressing
his cheek against the boy's wound. When that didn't
work, he lifted a fellow emergencer's open book right from
her linen lap, placing it atop his son. Heavy book, hardback. His

father, blood drying on his chin, on his wattle, his
work-shirt, pressed down, said, "You astonish me, B. Francis,"

said, as if B had cracked the book's first mysteries,
"Well, is it good reading?"

said, as if from inside the albumen of the book itself,
"You're seizing—he's seizing—someone come, someone come!"

The aide who netted B, said, "I have you!" pulling him forth
without lifting him from the flowing hospital tiles.

After the fisher released him, his father, crouching
near him, said to no one, "That'll never grow back."

Portage

He knew the bends here,
and knew well this one
from which a loud beating
sound came, the surrounding
farmland's own heart pumping.

Impassable,
       he said, ungrudging.
His oar asked the gunnel
to glide against a place
where we could unfold
and stumble out.

Dragging the weight
of the canoe over the bank,
he made a path of crushed
marsh-grass that I could
clamber up.

Follow me.
       Okay, I said, and
slipped on the muck,
my face close to
the sweet rankness.
I crawled before
standing, could
see that he was pleased
when I could walk.
I smelled my
hands, didn't wipe them
clean with the rag
he offered. I wanted
to wear this.

Bigger steps,
        he said, under sun
        more gentle than
        it had been in
        the ovening canoe.

        He pulled off his
        cap to let more
        world in. Across
        crop rows carved through
        by the creek, creatures
        bawled, but I couldn't
        discern—cows maybe—
        maybe ducks exploding
        from their weed-cribs
        far downriver—or
        kingfishers complaining—
        or straining tractor engines—

        and the systole sound
        of some hard-rhyming
        kind wheeling toward
        parched outermost
        unreachable terrain.

Down again,
        said my taciturn
        son barely audible
        through the stutter-
        thundering sound
        coming from the fields.

Steadying hand on
my shoulder, he waited—
to catch his breath, I
thought, or to check his
watch and calculate
the bends ahead.

Right on time.
  On time for what?
  I thought.

He skidded the keel
down the bank on
the logjam's other side.

He called me down,
guided me,
Step firm.
Don't sit 'til
you plant
your feet.

I wobbled, skated,
crouched, crashed my
ass on the bow seat,
gave thanks when
he, too, safely sat,
instantly settled,
paddled us into
the current.

And!
  My son, the orchestra director,
  raised his oar-baton above him.

And!

    I would not write
    with this child-heart
    if I had never lifted
    his limbs into the air
    and out of his onesie
    and his diaper
    and into another,
    if I had not
    cradled his head
    and opened his closed
    fists and kissed
    his tiny palms—

And!

    and, so, all the reaching
    palms I will encounter ever.

Now!

    The jetting irrigation spray
    slapped us with full-volume
    coldness—twice.

I would give, I tell you

anything to be a poem—they are a species four million years
in becoming—they won't line up—they cut in, they don't
accept the usual terms of extinction, won't resign to a sentence
of life imprisonment unless in solitary confinement—when
water has poured from the stone they drummed they drum on
the water or turn over the stone and skip it across their own
troubled skin—

they—I mean the poems—they   invent the ashglow, the
chainsaw, the impolite applause of branches, the stadium
benches and their stickiness, the kisses of subway fists and
elbows and their personal-space invasiveness, the drainpull,
the stamp of flipflops on the floor of city buses—they wear
chaps like I will never wear—the unrecycleable poets making
chapbooks humbler, holier than overfull books,   and
sometimes staplebound, sometimes with a splice string along
the spine—is it for tightening the thing when it slackens over
time?—what do you think?

—they invent the little fleshflap on the ear so that sound
sounds your skin before it goes in *keen*, a word rooted in kin
but kinda suggesting that they mourn   what their kind don't
hear.

Comparable miracles

You asked me what I thought Sam Sierra thought
that day I put him out—fifty years ago today.

Well, first, you've got to know I wanted no one to know—
and it was Sam who has told it and does still.
Mill laborers saved each other's asses over
and over through the years and didn't tell—why should we?
Hell, the real mystery is why Sam won't leave that day
go and give me some peace from making me his hero.
What's the deal that he thinks his saved life is a big deal?

He'll call me this afternoon and same as always
I'll say, Could we please talk about something else, Sam? Please?
And he will—he will—but not really—he'll tell me
about the anniversaries of his comparable miracles—
finding his lost car in the Walmart lot, or surviving an audit, or his
oldest returning from the newest war, his youngest from cancer—
wonders in which I had no part, except that Sam feels I do
because he wouldn't have lived to be saved again and again
if I hadn't thrown my jacket over the fire on him
made by the acetylene sparks arcing over his
shoulder and springing into flames small at first
and, just that fast, not—and big as fists, big as
pennants, big as whipping flags waved by ghosts.
At full sprint, I struck him off his stool, stuck
myself to him, his welding mask and mine still on,
and we rolled and spun and rolled for hours upon hours—

I thought he thought so too—though the time was
all in all about twelve seconds that we spent on
the ground until we sputtered out, smoked, rocked hard,
realized we had flung our heads off—well, I felt
he felt that also when we saw one ember made
of two men reflected in their—our—masks so far
away from us. Sam looked like me, I mean he looked
like he should let go, should stand up, should retrieve his
mask and torch, and check and clean them. Thanks, B, he said.

I said, Thanks, since for twelve seconds we were the same
man, the very same. Went to the locker room where we told our
foreman we were completely out and pretty much all right, agreed
to have the infirmary nurse certify us as cold ash, trashed
our damaged shoes, clothes, redressed, rejoined our crew, finished
our shift. Shit happens—and how. Every day we set ourselves
on fire. Some days we're not put out and other days we are.

You asked me to tell you what I should have let Sam Sierra
tell. I told—and I'm ashamed of myself now.

Awake, thinking himself asleep,

B saw one pale cottonwood
leaf tumble up, curve under
in the cold, mild current, glide down,
wet lace furling, autumn not

reappearing. Saw one brown trout
sipping black ants fallen from
eldest and uppermost branches

shivering. Saw one lingulate
dabbler landing on the surface
where an old-woman dragon-cloud swam
and became no one when he gazed
longer at her glaring blue eyes

closing. Felt one *hello*-strike shock
his tippet hard, dance upstream, shake
its head *yes* and *no*, spit the hook
in a galvanic loop-maneuver instant. Reeled
in and dropped the rod at his feet,

quietly laughed at his own sudden
hunger and leaden aloneness,
and tore open and read aloud
the ingredients list of his
last grease-glorious Slim Jim. Read
an entire love story carved
into a spellbound aspen:
Q&K4EVR—NOT

Love poem

We were climbing down from heaven
when you called.

Climbing up is slower now that
we are old.

Estivation

None of the people here
believe B when
he tells about
the drowned crow
stuck head and
breast in the
mouth of a
pond frog thrashing
to dislodge the
bird or to
swallow more down.

Seven years old
when B saw.

And now at
seventy he still
sticks by the
story, which will
not let him
go: the seizing
continuing for days;
the eyes-shut feasting
frog, dead or
dead-asleep; the crow's
body gorged on
by maggots, its large
wings spread wide
open in after-flight.

Could that memory
be outlived through
his repeated story?

Could B ever,
ever be believed?

Believe me—one
crazy regular like
him—a summer
customer—can ruin
your bar forever.

Mrs. Passerat transmits the gospel, 1968

(On April 4, 1968, the Reverend Martin Luther King
said to the musician Ben Branch: "Make sure you play
'Take My Hand, Precious Lord' in the meeting tonight.
Play it real pretty." They were his last words.)

Within the melody sing harmony
already there, the root you know you heard.
This way the other you you sing breaks free

and celebrates the ordinary day
of fruit maturing on old wood,
of melody that rings with harmony.

Make sure you sing "Take My Hand, Precious Lord"
and pray you reach far, far inside
so we hear how you, the other you, breaks free.

Pale foreign teacher teaches pale boy to try
to sing The Word inside the gospel word,
the harmony inside the melody!

All irony sounds some absurdity
we sang our younger yearning selves toward:
the you you sang in order to break free.

On every day you sing, bring it, bring it, boy,
sing pretty, sing pure like his friend Branch did.
Within the melody sing harmony:
this way the other you you sing breaks free.

Troubled guest

That one has come for me,
I said to myself, training for another
race, running distance
on a familiar trail
in desert ranchland.
Not far beyond me,
the tumbleweeds, the shape of
my private, accumulating
failures as the elderly
brother to my younger
yet elderly brother,
circled the barren depressions
or skidded down and out
on the slight inclines,
sometimes exploding into
each other and recomposing,
a body growing chaotically larger
and larger, the torso
ballooning, the friction
of rolling over heated
sand causing slight roundness
and thistledown lightness,
primordial nowness,
an awesome loft and
directionless acceleration. From
inside the one whistling
and crackling weed-carcass
came crowd-whispers,
came hymns, came
accusing prayers sung by
the cooling ashes of churches,
came one pilgrim
traveling one fire-path
running.

Nap

In late larval stage
she curled this leaf around her—
through cold wind she rocked

near her mother tree
from which stark shadows reached
and warm light-hours.

Other autumn scrolls
clustered around her, deepened
their sleep and hers.

You couldn't believe
her instinct for surviving
another season—

until you saw her
and her kind in their costumes—
bright testimonies—

until you witnessed
her veins of fire brightening
upon leaves greening—

until you pulled sheets
around you, entered again
the book Mother left.

Tilt-up

I'm on this construction crew building tilt-ups, and a fight breaks out over who said what to the crew boss who over and over again blamed all of us standing there with hammers at our belts or in our hands—a hazardous situation—but one of us has a nail-gun, the one who really is to blame, who actually told the crew boss everything that started the fight—he shoots nails—at close range—one spikes my helmet— two—the third pings off —the sound is not much different than a nun's long nails tatting a school desk—his bad aim pisses him off so he shoots at the hunting dogs and radio stations on high volume inside our windows-down parked cars—can't kill the sound of them—you can't win this fight against him until he almost not quite runs out of the speeding bursts of ammo nailing the hand you held up to the face you couldn't protect—he shoots at his own steel-toe boots under which were secrets he meant to stamp down— —you see a lot of them on these tilt-up crews—they were once arborists, a lot of them, and quite a few cosmologists, and some climatologists, pacifists who have always wanted their own nail-guns— —at the hospital where they had to pull my nailed hands away from my face, the doctor said to the nurse, "On 'Three' "—when no one asked what is a tilt-up I told the nurse all of four walls are built on the ground and tilted up to make a house—whose big idea that was I don't know—probably never will.

What I've got so far is

the sound of the cowbells outside
my open bedroom window at
the midnight hour when rising veils
upon veils of frog-calls muffle the
stem-shiverings and ground-tusslings
in these woods, my world beyond the
town, not far beyond, but giving
the illusion that no creature
necklaced in cowbells comes to ask
a round of unwelcomed questions
here, and another round, circling
on paws or cloven hoofs,
its shoulders and thick neck and lifted
head shifting, creating boned, jointed,
knuckled song to which I, like
a horror movie victim, can
only answer, "Hello? Hello?"

What I've got so far is "Hello?
Hello? What do you want?" I'm chained
to dark staining dark, to outside
quiet rubbing quiet my slack
old-man lungs, the cold-cooling cold.
The creature circles my home for
a way in, circles again, and
what I've got is the unwelcome
friend, that one friend who knows the ways
in, the lone companion for a man
as alone as I have been at
the window where my face confronts
my face, sorry as all jokers
on a card's slick surface. Pretty
much all I've got is the weight of
my life pressing me down, teeth sinking
in, eyes wide open, jaws locking.

What I've got so far is
a cowbell sound—a damned cowbell!—
at my end that will cause others
the inner smile or giggle or
restrained or unrestrained howling
laughter. Hello? Hello? Is my
hours-erasing last hour some bad joke?
Man dies fighting soap dispenser.
Man dies diving from Putt-Putt bridge.
Man fatally picnics at ax-throwing
contest for men in grief counseling.
Man in crowded bus asphyxiates
while giving CPR to dying
deflating realistic sex doll.
Man gilding giant Buddha topknot
plummets to next manifestation.
Man ingests ground glass, dies emitting
stunning, delicate cremation urn.

An afternoon in Troup County, Georgia

In order to suppress the flood's next rush
and the utter collapses coming with the fiercer
razing synchronous expulsions of rivers and
streams at their many crush-points, we tore
gravestones by the hundreds from our town's
Black cemetery. Holding the lichened faces
against our chests, we felt the runes of incised
testament, felt our soft chins settle upon
the unadorned heads of ossified stone.

Running to the flood-encircled school, we
trenched and bailed and timbered sections of
wall. We capped the whole high, round barrier
with the largest stones we found. We shoveled
up heaps of cemetery loam so we could bank the
magic enclosure we made around our fifty-four
grade schoolers, their amused, calm white faces
at the windows, hands waving, sure we had
saved them with our frantic salvage operation.

If we had not caused their deaths, if they
had lived, if any one of them had survived,
we would have heard them repeat all their
lives—and all our lives—The Legend of the
Rescue: of how a ring of ripped fence-boards
and grand gate-arches and chain-sawed ancestor
oaks and blocks of loam heaved from almost
unnoticeable berms throughout the vast
cemetery of our town's infernal others had been
carried by a swarm of heroic fathers and mothers in
seven hours' time. The legend would leave
untold our smug, fatal willfulness in ignoring
choices offered us for evacuating our children.

The story, we assumed, would praise, above
all else, our ingenious claiming of those
stones that we gambled could hold against the
flood boiling up inside the barrier, and,
by the minute, shifting elementally the
balance in the basement storage chambers,
foundation, superstructure, bearing walls,
and the perennially replaced roof of the entire
cheaply priced, freshly painted clay-brick place.

If our hearts had not drowned on that one
afternoon, it would have done them good to
hear the story's little epilogue—year after
celebratory year—about our admirable intention
to rebuild the cemetery, to replace the edifices we
salvaged, to make new berms, to restore
each stone and to place each one exactly
where it belonged, to plant new laurel
oaks, to reconcile ourselves with souls we
felt would understand our version, the proud
version we knew would be told by our
thrilled survivors, our oldest children, our
children's irreplaceable children, our own.

Another miracle in the life of Sam Sierra

Sam must have thought his cat was a traveler when
lost, because only two days after Mr. Cabbage went
missing, Sam and I put up fliers in all the nearest
neighborhoods and ones as far as half a mile from his
house. He must have believed a major campaign was our
best strategy, since we stapled and taped up hundreds of
Mr. Cabbage portraits, face shots endearing because, I
have to be honest, the face was more or less a
whiskered cabbage with lips and nose and eyes.

We started our posting at sunrise and worked
until sunset. 260 fliers—laminated because this was
ice storm season—large posters because of love—
because of awe, providing few words: HAVE LOST
MR. CABBAGE CALL SAM SIERRA—and it gave his
address and phone and email. When he is in
distress or absolute delight or is tapping his walking
cane on places in-between, I am Sam's assistant since I
live close and am longer lost and more irrecoverable than
most lost folks. And since Sam links me to his luck, he
calls me whenever good fortune has come already
or the same kind has again—you don't have to ask
him about the origins—he impulsively tells
everyone, and in every telling his newest miracle
reminds him of his first, in which he had An Angel—
that would be me—who confirmed for him "we all
have one." For the record, I will state that I have never said,
"Sam, let me remind you I am your Angel." I can
remember only one instance in which I did something
commendable for him—years ago—for twelve seconds.

On our search, I found out that an ice storm striking
pavement and cars and hedges and bare branches
can sound like a creature following you, invisible,
crying out. I found that angry people will come
growling from their homes in the worst possible
weather to make you pull down your flier from
anything they believe (usually falsely) is
their property. I found you can put them out: say,
"Look at that face," and point; say, "What if that was
your cat?" and take off your warm gloves and offer a
handshake; say, "Don't make me staple your mouth
shut, you jerk," standing close, loaded staple gun in
hand. I found that in every neighborhood at least
one person has a lengthy lost cat story that no
one until you has listened to all the sad way through.
Some few will tear down a flier like Sam's. More than a
few will check to make sure the flier stays.

Sam and I had not seen each other except for sandwiches
together when we met up, hands empty, our fliers having
constructed a far-reaching culture of Mr. Cabbages in the
dark everywhere around us. On our walk home Sam related
miracles he felt I should know about: how his younger
sister, in her late seventies now, had celebrated her fortieth
wedding anniversary by divorcing her abuser, and how her
abuser, who had once been our steel mill foreman, had
apologized to the wrong person—that is, to Sam—for
ruining Samantha's life, and asked what he could do,
and beat Sam up to show him how it's done, which Sam
considered fortunate because until that time he could
only picture her hellish days and hours and minutes as
abstraction. And did I hear that she had remarried? Did
I know that used canes are cheap? I had not, did not. Sam
said that Goodwill has a full bin of them, his face alight, his
stride more confident than mine over the black ice.

What did I think Sam thought when we got to his house
and Mr. Cabbage sat there full of himself on Sam's
doorstep? He must have thought what he said: "Mr. B has
saved us again," and held in his arms every pure hope a
human can hold, and petted it, and, eyes full of tears, said,
"Thank you." "No—thank *you*," I said to the prodigal cat.

Okay. There's more to tell that I don't need
to tell, since Sam will for sure. He will—he will.

But. Well.

The next day Sam walked among the vast populations
of Mr. Cabbages all afternoon and past sunset—the worst
of the ice storm sheeted him in gold and gray and the sky's
darkening green. He fell, skewing his ankle. His cane
skidded away. He retrieved it. Continued. With a black
grease pencil he wrote on every face: FOUND.

I know this. I know this because I, his
shadow, followed, almost hidden, caring, silent.

Ladder

I climbed down the
ladder into the empty
room, moonlight there
rippling over impact marks,
crater rays and
collapsed rilles where
Gideons and beer bottles had
been thrown, where my
thoughts' shadows flowed
over the round
rim, strode onto
the diving board, arrowed
into the shallow end.

In season, the Dive Inn was
full of baseball fans too cheap
to stay near the stadium.
Liquor store one block away,
an out-of-business Waffle House,
abandoned church, benchless,
treeless, pathless park.

Scorpions would fall in,
snakes, desert mice—once the
hollow carcass of a rabbit,
an owl's morsel, I guessed.
Small boy's underpants,
a nightgown, a lace thong,
shining new red silk
scarf pooling on the thirsty
drain, more than
half swallowed down.

The pool was never filled—I
had no choice. I had no
choice. Every summer I appealed to
the owner who, instead, made me
clean, patch, repaint, retile,
who wanted the green pool lights
polished, the filter system
refurbished, the rules on the
giant sign touched up
with shiny black paint, and the
self-locking gate latch replaced.

Every steaming summer when
the angry hotel guests
saw me there and
asked, I answered in
the owner's cruelest voice,
"What do you care?"

He cast upstream again, mended

line for dead drift, let it unwind, pass him,
stall out behind. He slipped a wet river
stone into his hand, walked, kicked rubble,
waded deeper in to find another stone spilled
from a socket, tricked from a magic
well, a second pulsing need.

His fist closed around his secrets. He
breathed into them, lifted, tested their
weight, stone skins, stone sweat, stone blood,
core, seed. A different man might pitch the
stones across the river, skip or slingshot
them over the reflected web of first stars.

He kissed, bit his rich portions,
worked his spit around them, whistled
once through the wet tongues,
swallowed his prizes. Could not breathe
when both loves sunk down into
him. Could not move in the
cold river. Could not leave.

What a Dancer Does

What makes the engine go?
Desire, desire, desire.
The longing for the dance
Stirs in the buried life.

Stanley Kunitz, "Touch Me"

Thanksgiving

You said a farmer's file worked best,
and lightly raked the double-cut
face over the outside edge of my
bare wrist where beads of blood
at once swelled up so fast that

I couldn't begin to imagine you
would use the single-cut face to
finish this edge of me, filing much
more deeply and slowly this ruby gash
I still wear: my heirloom cufflink.

You wiped the file, reached for
my empty, small hand and bared
your farmwoman's muscled arm
and gave your wrist to me, smiled
your grand grandmotherly smile.

On certain days when new injuries
answer old wounds, I give thanks
for your calm instructions, Grandmother,
the two keen methods for showing
myself as I am to my grandchildren.

Smiles mark my two cruel faces when
I teach my brood of tender ones how
they can be sharpened and can sharpen:
I bare their wrists and my scarred wrist. I
provide implement and initiation.

You are my feed.

I've learned to love the face of that word.
And in my feed
strange coincidences have occurred:
whenever I'm addressed as a friend
my distant but beloved acquaintances write *fiend,*
my best and my longest-loved dearest ones write *frnd.*

I feel no need
to ask if they really know that I am the weird
threatening visitor from their appalling dreams,
broken-winged shadow falling upon his victims,
crozier-headed cobra knelling the air twelve times
before uncoiling his mystery and striking.

Why should I need to ask what friends mean?
Why ask about what they have written?

If I am your friend
then I am your feed.

The Bronze Level

When our dancing bounced
the water in the
marble-glass pitcher,
parallelograms
of light strobed the walls
and the ceiling for
time-spilling seconds.
Laughter inside light!

A swiveling step,
learned in our newest
lesson, sent weirder sun
in cyclone arms
elapsing into
the pitcher bottom.

A tree stem's clawing
shadow slowly stirred
and trembled
the liquid and entrained
spinning particles,
reassembled them—treble
hooks everywhere!

We splashed, we
circled, we circled
there. We struck.

Interrupting Issa's nap,
sparrows sing and call—
an old man amidst them says,

"Inside the full sleeves of snow
worn by your Jizō tree
I glimpsed the sanctuary

of auroral light
that now dances through me, and
will after I fall."

Issa bows, answers,
Glimpsed what, you say? I'm dreaming
this—and so are you.

Click & drag to look around

Steam released from the
opened dishwasher.

> Her hair moistening.
> And her eyes. And his.

> > Darkness   outside, lawn
> > stillness, gray coldness.

> Why not a kitchen dance? Why
> not spin once to change places?

> > Why not answer the
> > wind pounding the door?

> Why not a thieves' toast, a kiss
> of their stolen I-HOP cups?

On glossing not yet icing
windows: frozen spider script.

> Never-quitting-stuttering
> fridge overproducing cubes.

> > Space-age toaster. Charred sunburst
> > oven mitts. Ice-age breadbox.

Loose floor tiles, wobbly
lazy Susan.

> Matching pinstripe aprons balled
> on the butcher-block counter.

Why not stare into the clean plates one
by one while the heat is leaving them?

        Why not glue Santa's beady stream-stone eyes
        back on—a new candy cane in his hand?

                Why not lift the green ribbon
                into the book's Bake section?

Radicle

for Chris Hale

I had not seen sunlight cut
                    and slice and strike through my
                                own trees in my own woods
in the emerging stages
                    of the brisk days that I had
                                not read as astonishments
of new hope arriving
                    in the brightest forms that
                                I had not named as songs in
the simplest prayers sung by
                    the sun's swift promisings that I
                                had not once noticed in
the swerving blades of their
                    flowing immensities or
                                their fire-whetted arrow tips
that struck cleanly through me
                    to this opening seed
                                I might have become all
along had I learned that I
                    could write my life here with
                                you in the emergence and
be singing-green words
                    releasing-green
                    and piercing-green

                                greening

Mrs. P: a lesson on warming the voice

"Oh, here in my heart,
I still believe
We shall overcome some day."
Joan Baez rendition, "We Shall Overcome"

Find where the sparks come from
by breathing like a newborn.
Find what the fire will become

inside you when you have formed
from sparks one flame stirring sound.
Find where the sparks come from,

furnaces within that hum
in your body, the faint amen
found when the fire will become

rounder, rounder in volume,
when fire's brief intonations
find where the sparks come from.

Softly sing. Call, call the warm
returning to you as a tune.
To find what the fire will become,

sing softly. Softly assume
the sound of your origin.
Find where the sparks come from.
Find what the fire will become.

The Man Rose

You must admit:
I smell good.

If hellebores have opened
I rub them on.

When peony trees bud and
azaleas fir I
lean down to be painted with
their moist newness.

You are good-smelling,
say people who
are pleased for me,
an always newly scented man.
What is your cologne?
they ask who long to be
cologned in this way.

I rub on haiku poems
that lightly cling to the page.
Crushed peppercorns.
Crushed cosmos blossoms.
Crushed walnut flesh.
In certain moods, I wear
the curry powders
from fragrant envelopes.
According to impulse:
seats popcorn-buttered in theaters,
soft crumbs on café tables, on
chair bottoms and arms,
vape-trails in open air markets
and worm containers on
the dust-gunked shelves of
marina fridges.

Your jaw and neck are
mysteriously stained, people say
who wish more men
were stained as I.

In pollen season
each car in the parking
lot wears a coat
of oak and poplar
and lilac dust
and a film of carwash soap
in fabulous flavors,
and the trace
of lemony and cherry wax,
of mango-strawberry-banana rinse.
I apply myself to
your hoods and doors, to
the fragrant peduncles of
your car mirrors. If
your clothing has been
infused with after-death care
I scrum-hug you in
your coffin, rub my cheeks
against your perfumed hands
at peaceful rest, your
face vernix-myrrhed as when
you were newborn.

I trust that you understand
I must wear you in
your season. And when
your season has passed.

I smell good:
you must admit that
your nose
remembers me.

I am the man
about whom you
say, *That man lingers,*
doesn't he?

Seating chart

        Now is not the time to
        raise your glass.

Perversely, you have placed me
and other divorced and
drunken members of this
wedding party in seats between
the newly betrothed couple.

As usual, I bring so little to
give that a prosperous-looking
guest near me, well-suited—and,
well—stoned, just asked someone,
"Man, where is this guy from?"

Do I know how to answer that question?
Does the Devil know how to row?

        Please stay seated.
        Put your glass down.

I've always left the calm and
slow chaos of Between
in order to live inside
ludicrous conditions of
sheer height and expanse.

When Between has crashed
shivering waves over
Rock, I've caught the
lovers' talk knocking at
bright, sealed walls of shells.

I've worn them around my
neck, and brought them with me.

When Between has flooded
Hard, I've gathered
splinters of drowning
vows and sinking shards
of holiest holy ceremony.

I've brought them, too—
see how they fall from me?

I'm glad I could bring these
gifts in celebration of you.

(What else could I bring
but Will, that marital crevasse
between Unless and Until.)

Look at us. Look at them,
at our children's daring choices.

       Do not raise your glass.
This is not the right time.

Play "White Rabbit"! Play "White Rabbit"!

You will always make your same damn request and
I will always only play my own music:
that's, more or less, our solemn nightly contract.

Before I lay down the last bars of my song,
I'll point you out in the thin crowd to stick
my glory to you, to make your request ours.

I'll hold the notes so we two will share the long
diminishment of sound-fires warming us,
so that together we call for last-call peace.

I'll wait until you raise your glass and can stand
unsteadily and tilt sloshing love towards me
and the remains of the audience that remains.

You will bow deeply, your hair sweeping the floor.
I will raise the tip jar and, by habit, ask,

Hey, Alice, tell me—did I come pretty close?

Prose poem by God

I could not address your questions in the form in which you asked them. 9) Touched the sores through the linen wrappings. 8) Dry Creek Flood Zone. 2) Algal bloom. 7) Failure Semantics. 4) DIY transubstantiation. 1) Endangered tongue. Fossil evidence. Labyrinth of ruins. 5) I, the bright & mourning star, the spirit & bereft bride, the prophet & plague, have sent mine broken angel to testify unto you these things in the burned churches. 6) Sublime malabsorption. 3) Yoke gets in your eyes. 10) Requested bad directions. 4) Bones, said Adam. No bones, said Eve.

Gemels

is the name for trees
like us, growing in

the same production
job in such close

quarters that we join
root, trunk, branch.

When you say, "Make a pear,"
together we bear the fruit.

When I say, "Let the flesh be sweet,"
together we sweeten.

Who doesn't fight the fusing of
skin and torso and phloem?

We fight—of course we do.
Of course. Our fighting has

inosculated us into
warring singular impulses.

Who doesn't resist bearing the other's
fruiting, dimming, dying process?

We complain,
just as you'd guess.

I say, "What 'us'?"
You say, "Your place or mine?"

The dividing bitterness between us
pours out as laughter conjoined.

As laughter, yes. Together we
wear our wearing out,

our sloughing off,
our bowing down.

At the time of
our final harvest

you ask,
"Will we bear this?"

I ask,
"Will we bear this?"

For us, the last kiss
will come all at once.

A golden ratio day

In
these
rectangles
of
rainwater:

Our
faces
trembled
spiraled
there:

your
hands

You.
　　　Weren't
　　　we
　　　lovely?
Me,
too.

Rainclouds:
three

held
mine.

II

The daylight waltz

Our instructors   are displeased.
Something we   are doing
we must not   ever do.
I hold my   dance frame, keep

air as I   should between
my arms and   ribs to float
not freight me   before you.
Something has,   however,

caused a brief   critical
straight twinkle   danced by our
vigilant   instructors.
Our four points   of contact

must be   fully correct:
my hand high   upon your
left shoulder   blade, your hand
opened at   my shoulder

and arm joint,   thumb balanced
at the right   connection
of arm that   rests lightly
against arm   at proper

formal and   romantic
waltz height, right   hand nested
cordially   in the V-
tilt at the   juncture I

have formed with   my left palm
held in a   boy's greeting
no higher   than the top
of your relaxed   woman's shoulders.

As Mr.　　Allen left-
turns-left-turns　　Mr. Trautman,
I wonder　　how, how we
triggered their　　so-slight ice-

capading　　gesture of
displeasure.　　Not looking
down (Dance Sin),　　I can feel
my right shoe　　on the mark

at elbow's　　length, arrowed
between your　　feet subtly
flexed in half-　　heel matte blacks
perfectly　　correct and

neither far　　apart nor
too, too close　　together.
Seventy, like　　us, our two
instructors　　are, of course,

veering some　　from the lane
of second　　measure where
their rise and　　fall become
rise and rise,　　their right turns

are not right,　　not at all.
I have to　　wonder if
your anklet　　may be their
point of stress,　　your light cha-

cha-ing beads　　spoke-clicking:
incorrect　　incorrect.
We do not,　　in general,
offend the　　silence—we

are beyond   what Misters
Trautman-Allen   call "that
    fatuous   pillow-talk
phase" of the   dancers who

must whisper   "Slow-quick-quick,"
or "Turning,   now—Turning,"
or "Now—our   Progressive,"
or the worst,   "Open to Dip."

We know The   Dip, which should
not be called   "Wedding Dip"
("Why limit   it?" he asks,
and never   call him *Traut*),

needs only a   wide turn,
needs your waist   under my
unstraining   left arm, my
right arm and   wrist, my hand

raised in a   sword-flourish,
your wrist, your   hand up and
fingertips   in classic
rising-flame   lightness. And

all this to   only be
named *Dancing*   if wordless.
Why has—why,   I ask, has
our Mr.   Trautman now

so wrongly   miscountered
Mr. Allen's   left-right sway?
They have turned   out, in an
inexact   quarter-turn

to glare at   you, at me.
At least we're   not lipping
lyrics, that   high waltz-crime
Misters   Trautman-Allen

detest. We   can resist
stylizing   our fine head
movements   like the other
slack-neckers,   mouth-puckered

pistoners,   boob-bobbing,
board-pizzling,   penguining
rain-sippers   —we are not
clueless to   the proper

projection   of buttocks,
at least, at   very least.
There was once   a Mrs.
Trautman—Joan   —Joanna—

we do not   mention her,
Joanna,   Joanna—
trying to   sustain our
vertical   position,

the closing   of our feet
walk-waltzing the   motion,
our leg swing,   Joanna—
compression,   Joanna—

Joanna   —Joanna.
Twenty-eight   or thirty
thoughts of   her per minute.
The minutes must   be glided

past—better   concentrate
on our next   rotations
than once more   contemplate
Joanna's   line of dance

or other   Joanna
tragedies: uncontrolled
lowering   of backward
step, poor feet   trapped under

Joanna's   rear bumper.
Her shoulder   balance wrong:
our strongest   theory.
The balance   will not be

corrected.   The balance
is always   created
alone.   And all of his long
life, Mr.   Allen had

but one   partner, named
Helen—   or Helena—
but no wife.   Helena's
sense of the   tempo was

so perfect,   and perfect
her impact, her   recorrection.
In films, in   photographs
of them, she   is the day

of his day-   light. Shining
Helena   —Helena.
There is a   test at the
end, and one   must show one's

respect, one   must. One must
     actually   not reverse,
and one must   not progress
     simply. The   leader will

follow and   will trust how
follower   trusts and leads.
One who will   follow needs
     to give the   appearance

of no will,   but must—on
the lines of dance   —quiet
(quiet as the moon   )—pull.
Leader must   heed partner,

     within him   gyroscope-
like smoothness   responding
     to rising,   falling waves
that roll-curl   and that rip.

Mid-measure   they have stopped
dancing. They   clasp hands in
near-distance   closeness that
     waltzes. Oh,   Joanna,

Helena,   how our dour
instructors   have becalmed
us, waiting for   stillness
in our hearts   before they

will break the   dance silence.
We do not, of   course, of
course not, look   close at them.
We know well   enough that

our two   professionals
transfer and   transfer, that
neither one   rests himself
on both his   feet, ever.

"These few boards   are—are an
ocean," says   Mr. Allen.
"An ocean,"   says Mr.
Trautman, voice   glistening,

and he says, "Re-   member—
here—*here* you   are dancing
conversion—   not—*tell them*—"
"—destruction,"   says Mr.

Allen.   "Not destruction."
One turns the   other now
with almost   Viennese
boldness—they   fly free, our

instructors—   they arrive
at transitions with   their arms
sliding down   and off each
other—their   hands clasp—one

goes under   the other's
arm and he   rotates left—
one counter-draws   so that his
lover's strong   shoulders press

against his   chest, so his
instructor's   head inclines
closer to   instructor's
face, and the   double-hinge

of their hands   recapitulates
the wordless   spin that will
make us learn   how dancers
could always say   more about

what was, what   is—if words
were what a   dancer does.

III

The River Scratch

Selfie

Larger than life-size, with
rotating heads and necks, with
rattles in their eyes, our
pretend-owls and plastic
hawks mildly entertained the
starlings puncturing the
siding of our home.

An Ace friend advised a
system of tall dowels with
long and longer
streamers the slightest
breezes would send up as
snake simulacrums to
terrify the bird-pests.

The agent marketing our
home suggested her
prosperity church sell us
six foul-smelling cheeses in the
shape of Jesuses, His arms
raised in impatient anger
at the expensive invaders.

Hems-first, the birds bit our
Christ down, desecrated
His creations, owl, hawk,
snake, and came in numbers
great as pilgrim hordes to the
site where our lost cause
named all we owned.

This story will not end
well, our agent said,
called our home a
tear-down and our land a
plot, defined our story as a
glass half-full and us
blessed lilies of the field.

We burned down our home
then, poisoned our land,
fed the deadly ash to our
wandering children and
their wan children, and
ate of it and them in a
satisfying, brief feast.

And neither do you now
harvest or sow,
she said, who could not
suppress her smile,
who called for a picture to
show us—and her—victorious.

January 6, 2020

Oh, that.

We've hung the bell inside
because we want that copper-green
mouth and forked tongue above
us to faintly sing whenever
someone lets weather in.

Don't apologize, dear
friends. Leave the door open.

Oh,
that.

Death.

Death.

December 15, 2020

Tribute

During the final rites for the nation,
I tried not to love and to weep for,
tried not to ask for God's mercy on
poor Mr. Rudy Giuliani.

Hair dye leaked down and onto Rudy's
chin and cheek, and ringed his upper lip—
but not until he lowered his head and
gooily yipped, did I recognize
my bottled self in my family
lineage of drunks with grand sailing
ships inside that had taken youthful
journeys and never again left dock.

See, I said to the Rudys I've known,
That—*that*—is how addiction wrecks our
brains and hearts with such breakneck speed we
can't know who we are or were or where
we might have been before we were not
even recognizable human
beings capable of calling out
for rescue—you can't remember how
many rescuers you've already
drowned, how you've utterly forgotten
your arms belonged to you, to others
too—how all your own helping words and
your words for seeking help have gone—and
you want retribution for how you've
been judged—and you stand at a bar in
an imaginary court and you
trot out your griefs about fraud but you
cannot quite pronounce the word, Rudy,
freudulent fuckwad who drools, sprays, spits
venom as if you could be rid of

it, who pisses on anyone who
remembers you before you became
this sweating garbage-spilling golf bag—

I testified to all this at some rapturous
last call: That, I said, is me—I mean—
I mean the mayor-of-nothing you—
that is how you ooze, drag your smeary
self over rehabbed fictions of you
decomposed and gelatinizing.
Now everyone can see you are
servant to the clown-king marking your
self-owning kneeling condition and
in one phlegm-sucking grunt owning you—
everyone can see the starving swamp
creatures trying to find a way out
of your eye-sockets or over the
collapsing walls of you—that cribbed child
way you move in your cage, everyone
sees—the mumble-speak that was once your
heroic defender's megaphone
shout, everyone hears—the smell of your
silt tie and untucked shirt and sticky
dark suit—everyone smells you from a
distance of six feet more than the six
required by the pandemic moment—
everyone tries hard to unsee you
celebrate yourself with your hand on
your mitchy puckered slowpoke dick.

Of course I mean it, every word—
of course I know—I know none of what
I can say can cure or kill or will
or ever could this pain that is his

and mine, our treason upon treason
upon treason against what we might
have been. He's given in to himself
so much he has no hope of giving
up—look at the dribbling fuck who has
fucked up the simple ability to
know what flows from him, to speak without
that vomit lip-cover gleaming on
his pouting lower lip, sagging neck.

I've got to find a meeting somewhere.

Did I know you, Rudy? Do I? If
I do, you will have to let me go.

November 19, 2020

At 70

An hour's work,
the rummy told the initiate,
cost you thirty.
Said,
For his own sake
I take this limb off and
those lower ones—off—
I take off that high
crown—gotta take
off that dozen there—
unstable—I clear out the
center—clear out the dead,
the dry, I clear up that
cross-growth—see?—not
pretty—nothing pretty about
a mulberry tree, you ask me—
truth is, I should make
firewood of him, but what
would he add up to, how
long would you burn that
guy?—some idiot put him
here—what, seventy years ago?

He's sure no apple
tree, am I right?—boreworms
got him good, must've been
last year—they call them
angel grubs—I take off all
that stressed wood
(hell, that's half
the tree)—no wings,
but heaven-white, those bores—
beautiful really—really, a tree
so wormed up—that's a good
living end—brings birds from

everywhere—hundreds sometimes—
the one time in his life he's a full
buffet—think of all the little free
meals for all the screaming mouths
in the nests hereabouts.

Mr. Shamsi, the man who
taught me pruning, was my friend, too—
my teacher—I called him Shams—
never owned his own tools—
sold and had and sold them—
told me and Sal—gone, gone also—
said the best death a tree ever
gets is being borne away this way.
Shams said some of the
stupidest, truest things—he said
a tree that good-doomed can watch
himself scooped out by dreamers,
dreamers scooped out by singers
returning later for
more—he said the tree can hear
how their singing gets louder—
wilder.

Cairn

Alone at river crossings I privately ask
that I may start my life from scratch.
I'm grateful no one can hear
my voice sounding any different than
the murmuring surface carrying
brisk shadows of branches and
birds downstream, sun-stunned clouds
that have been
            glimmering there.

            That's the scream of a hawk,
I told my two boys. That's the cry
of prey. The tearing of meat.
Here—two last sticks of gum. Make
them last. Sweet!—am I right?
With smaller steps, we'll stumble
less. (We could cut our lawn by
walking through with all those
burs on our
            shoes and socks.)
        In your hair is pollen enough for
two pollen-bombs. Don't set them off
by singing the wrong rock song. Let's
not clean our glasses while the air is
so golden. Squint to see if your
eyes change your questions. Look—on
the back of your own hands:
you're turning to dusk.
            (Only joking!)
        Try one more cast before we go.
This I guess is not the time or place for
us. Wasps live here! The kind in the petroglyphs.
Leave wasps alone. They build in rain—they'll
mistake us for storms. We'll make a cairn at
this crossing, so next time we

can see how the river took it down
or shook the stones but
                        let them stand.
            And anyway, snakes live here. Snakes!
Some people say they come in groups of six
and eight as a matter of habit. Some say,
"That's bullshit!" (Don't say "bullshit," okay?)

And, see, they make a raking shape in
the leaf-ghee mud whenever they
return to this bank where their young
            were born and were borne away.

If it's clear where you are

The black mask of death had become the proper one to wear during the newest iteration of viral nationalism. And in the holiday picture the losers bit back for one shutter-second the words they needed to say about the hacked Dominions, the unjust twitterverse, the vax apocalypse, the leftist Communist Democratics killing Christmas in Georgia. With no place to rest, the group felt this was the right time to pull off their masks, to fire up the back porch chimenea, pull out their too-short roasting sticks, toss their red maga-scarves round their necks, pour gasoline over one another—male grandchildren and great-grandchildren first—and pledge allegiance to the fire with which they poked their bulging eyes out, marshmallow oozing, the wool wicks aflame under their chins, delicious poison cocoa waiting for them.

B emailed Rooks to ask was he on the jobsite for the holidays.

Rooks wrote: Jupiter and Saturn were visible here just after sunset a few days ago. They were about as far apart as the angular diameter of the moon. Tonight they are a fifth that far apart, the closest they've been in several centuries, but it will be cloudy here, again, as it has been the last couple nights. If it's clear where you are, look for the brightest object over the western horizon, well to the right of the moon, and its dimmer companion, and give them my regards.

Why Owen Park

To shoot baskets
to blow my harp
to walk to walk

to blow my harp
to shoot baskets
is why I went there

and to laugh
with a whoosh
and to sing to sing

with my breath
is why and
to talk to talk

with my boots
shooshing path
made of gravel

mixed with chips
made from trees that
once ringed the pond

once cast crowns
made of shade
of trembling shade

when they
still when
I

still when
I still
lived

is why

Mrs. P: *the practice of* creaky voice

Tell me—tell me that your sweet love hasn't died.
Give me—give me one more chance to keep you satisfied.
Willie Nelson rendition, "Always on My Mind"

Your morning voice always creaks.
You wake with crying, you creak—
and creaking is singing that speaks.

Again: *Tell me.* Your voice aches
with what it cannot speak.
Your morning voice always creaks,

a soft, raw cry that awakes,
ascending now, still weak.
And creaking is singing that speaks.

Tell me. Tell me. Hear? It makes
a beauty that breaks music.
Your morning voice always creaks,

rocks noisily and squeaks,
reminds you life's comic,
creaking singing speaks,

reminds you that singing cracks
you open wider each practice,
since your mourning voice always creaks,
since creaking is singing that speaks.

Stacey Abrams returns to Troup County, Georgia

I work here
at night, on my
knees, headlamp
shining over the
unprotected beds
of roses despairing
too long in the county's
Founders Garden.

Reconstructing
the edifice of the
grand building
of justice, men have
wrapped, for shame,
the whole pale
monster in white
mesh netting.

Of all the ghosts in
southern counties
this one is now
the scariest: creaking
hooded belfry, layers
of webbing luffing
in the slightest
breezes, no light behind
the almost-hidden eyes.

I call my stubborn,
struggling enterprise
Resurrection.
I specialize in
Small Orchards
& Gardens, Outdoor
Altars, Home Cemeteries,
riven, burned.

My Sunday
ad explains my
odd work shift:
All resurrecting
done nights only.
Better to have
The Work seen
than The Worker.

I lightly rock
the roses from their
dry cradles
of dead earth. From
each I remove
all but the main
canes that I
trim close to the
root ball.

They need to be
bathed in
warm water and
returned to
renewed soil, their
roots seated firmly,
their fine root
hairs combed down.

In shock from long
thirst, they drink
as if awful
drunks recalling
and madly recovering
the rehydrating taste,
the return of
sunlight hunger.

Some nights I've
walked six miles to
return to the
sites of perennial
destruction. I
kneel down,
down close,
to this work that
is never done.

Who tries to
murder us in our own
land under our own
sun every time we lift
the blooms of our
risen selves to light
our shrouded,
dim nation?

From dawn to dusk
we will set
ablaze the hours
in this garden with
the giving-fires
that we will
pass along
for generations.

March 7, 2021

12 doorways

When a leaf shadow drifts over the ground,
you're standing on your own bones.

When it will not steal sunlight,
no flower blooms, no fruit ripens.

When you dream that you have a twin,
you'll lose a familiar within.

When you repair a thing you've broken,
look around you for something that needs breaking.

If you dream of doorways with no doors,
do not walk forward.

If you dream of doors
open in doorways, do not walk forward.

If you walk forward in dreams
you'll awaken.

When you repair a child who isn't broken,
you're a child who shouldn't have more children.

When your shoes are gone
you're done walking.

When your butt is cold
you're done smoking.

When you can't find your own roots growing,
you soon have none.

If the wind puts out your candle, light another.
If your second candle puts out your other—

Oh, Brother! Oh, returning Brother!

Descriptions of Heaven

Got your note
from the canyon—
glad to know you're
there again.

& why go
so often now?

Old as I am, I've
never been there
since, well, forever—&
can you and I imagine or
remember then?

I don't imagine I've
ever gotten such
fine descriptions of
heaven from you
even when you
were bringing your
school drawings home,
sixty years back.

Glad to have your
note about that
chilling warming
canyonlight, those well-
marked morning paths,
evening stars raining,
tent walls wiffling in
wind, taste of campfire
smoke, coals murmuring,
your own foot odor, your
back creaking, your
pencil screeching
in the quietness.

I'm going where your
words take me. Glad to
follow them alone so
far down, far in, beyond
our estranged distance.

Once you brought
home a drawing of your
pretend dad, who
crowded the small
sheet with his greatness.
You said his name
was *Goddam*, my
favorite expression
at the time. A mighty
man, his big hair
high, big eyes and
mouth smeary with joy.
His strong arms too straight
for elbows. His fingers,
ten on each hand,
long as rays of
sun or lightning.

The thing's still taped
to the fridge. Come see.

Rose

I knew but hardly knew why my mother brought the mild, bare miniature rose inside for winter and shelved it at the window that it faced in summer when she floated the same wild, small plant in an outdoor hanger fixed by picture wire onto a rotating device she had placed there years earlier in the eaves. Each time she watered this world, she pinched off dead and dying leaves and blossoms and stems, and closely inspected them with her fingers, pressed them into pockets so that later she might touch longer. I knew but hardly knew how such replete relapsed lives could matter. At every watering and tending session she turned the rose, turning another changing face toward sun, turning again and again—I knew but hardly knew how many times she had done this when I asked her once if the rose got tired of the spinning. In response, she took up my arms, said nothing at all, nothing, nothing, but raised my hands and fingers in the air, raised her own, and turned me, spun me hard toward, away from, toward her, spun me in her arms and hands and fingers in the loving-giving I've known and have hardly known since then in the remembering seasons.

Once, walking

Once, walking with my son Ed, both of us in our waders,
I said, "Well?" He said, "Feeling lucky?"

I said, "Never.
Always."

He gazed down into the water we were about to cross.
Not yet forty, he is a man who can read

the subtle fatal powers of rivers
as if from inside the embroidered cloths,

as if under the spell of the spreading,
shifting, splintered light of sun,

the lanterns inside the riverbed's larval cradles,
as if enacting their harrowing milliseconds-long

self-explosions of culminating pain
and desire at the river's surface.

Seventy soon enough, I share his skill in
reading the knotted grain of the sentence

formed by the flooded-full or thirsting streams,
by the slipstream's dispossessing shadow-ghostings.

I commit to the next step down and in
while guesstimating

the potentialities of hiddenness,
the face flowing beneath the face.

When he was a teen he had taught me fly-fishing.
He had learned from a master named Mr. Maybe

who could lightly pin a size-22 dry
to the bank upstream of him

where the slightest wrist-flick would unfasten
it onto the glimmering target of the trout feeding there.

(I irresponsibly fictionalize. But not about this matter:
Mr. Maybe. And my name, B, politely echoing his.)

The silken vapor over the river's surface silvered.
A good bright-morning death hour.

I said, "So."
"So. Every step'll be . . ." He did not have words.

He meant, *tremendous.*
He meant, *treacherous.*

I am proud to be his father. The day swiftly passed
when he might have been proud to be my son.

What was the question I would not ask?
What was the question he would not?

We will cross over again.
We will return.

He had taught me to position my feet upriver
though not directly. He had taught me to bend

at the knees in order to drill my weight down,
to watch for the next single step forward and

to recalibrate the specific goal of the bank ahead,
to let fullness of thought and feeling overwhelm doubt.

He had taught me to hold my arms slightly away from
my body, hold them firmly as a standing surfer must,

or a tray-aloft waiter. The position felt and looked
odd, and the oddness was pleasurable.

What was the question he could not ask?
What was the question I could not?

At the age of seventeen, I had obsessively worn
down to physical ruination a poetry anthology,

The Voice That Is Great Within Us, and I had
the confounding romantic convictions

of a fireman-arsonist when I vowed my inscribed
but unscarred life to my art at that early, clueless age.

From the first innocent step in, I wobbled, I counter-wobbled, I
faced directly upstream and was pulled down to my knees. The flow
spun, unfolded, tumbled, thrashed, wrung me, filled my clown
costume, soaked, boiled, sunk me. I wrote like a drowning boy.
The spitting, sucking flow burred me against the bottom. Submerged
whetted tree shreds rip-skinned my forearms, hands and fingers.
Undercurrent rabbit-punched me with its many fists.

Soused out of my dreamy head, I wrote, senseless,
directionless. During the half mile of river time—
instantaneously becoming a cork and a lead shot
—I thought I could hear someone, some one,
some other, an unrecognizable self
shouting for help in a weirdly exalted voice.

I would not land if I tried to land.
I would be brought if I would give in to being brought.

I have overdramatized. I sound like a person who insists on
fixing the bigger handle to the handle that fits.

*

"Feeling lucky?" my son had asked. That small part
of all of this account is accurate. Probably.

Probably not.
Probably not.

He has got the rhythm of how to live.
I have lived without that,

making what I have called "strides"
two stumbles at a time,

a miscast for every cast,
a misreading of the strikes.

The river's story of washing a man clean is, by far,
a story larger in scale than a man's story of crossing.

My son's laughter is purest
when he laughs at his father.

"Shouldn't we go home?" I ask,
undrained and sloshing in my fishing costume.

"Home?" he asks.
Nothing I will ever write

will ever cause more delight
for anyone than I can cause my son.

He laughs. How he laughs!
There is no question,

absolutely no question that
this river—this *is* his home.

Often, though less and less often,
I have returned to tread the same water
without him. I have imagined a younger me—
running in full stride downriver, weeping,
tearing through brush, absurdly hoping to outpace
the river's crushing forces—
a younger me determined to catch
that ludicrous old drowning man
in order to save him from his choices.

Sycamore

Waiting Christless day after Christless day there
in the sycamore tree Zack and B knew they had just
missed what they had come to understand might
have been a kind of joyful coming, but could be
only a cold Barton Springs sunrise when time
is owned by the blackbirds who watch, who wait to
signal what will swim the air each hour without a catch
and what will rise with the early light and drift up
and stir the fumes above the water and send them on
like the dying watching, waiting to give praise.

        In his warning voice B's dad had told the two, Oh
nothing on earth is like the boiling, radiating life
and the combustions of song and light at our spring. How
will you need or lose the slow-growing need of the Great I
Am? How will you find how much you are loved
without loving yourselves the warming light on your
cold arms and faces and on the sycamore's cold
sleeves when your eyes fill with coin-flowers that spring
from dark mounds broken by the golden spades of mornings.

        So I will have all the time I need?
asked B, asked Zack, reaching up again for
the highest hands reaching down for them, budding.

Finches

The Inception of Memory experiments were
conducted on zebra finches because their
vocal developments correspond to human
stages of encoding memories of notes. Young
birds were separated from their fathers
before encoding. The neuron
activities in the Nif brain region
were manipulated so that song
information sent to the HVC brain
region could be observed.

      He handwrote this found poem
on a postcard. On the other
side he asked if I ever planned
to sing about my sister or
brothers, my dad or mother, or
sing about my sons. Or my head
wound, or my nation, or lost friends.
Or Zen (which he, knowing of
my fallen Catholicism, called "Zin")
or my garden that he named
"B's goddamn Eden."

Or him.
Or him.

Laboratory finches do, he wrote, and
added, *Then they are incinerated.*
Yours,
H

What a Dancer Does

The parable of the table

The table turns! said
the son to his
father, and spun his
old man's resemblance on
the clean round surface
of the outdoor tabletop
that bright, brief afternoon.

O, stop, said his
father. O, dear son,
stop. But his son,
as sons must, turned
him old turned him
old turned him old.

Son and father set
their cups down on
the father's sunken sockets,
on his broken frown.

They scooted their chairs
forward and back, which
did no good since
their neighborhood was a
hilly place and steep,
in a seaside town
of empty pockets and
deep, where every man
and every man's son
killed his drinks before
they would spill, his
food before it would
slip, killed their time
together before they would
part, killed the words,

the few words that
could have splashed out.

The evening came then
as evening will, to
pour the last light
before the last call.

O, stop, his son
said. O, Light, stop.

The moon's dry ocean
bed replaced the old
man's grit and dust,
erased erased erased all
remnants of the sad
young man's old-man
face on this spinning
table in this seaside
town, on this hilly
and steep place.

The fit of some thing against somethings

The
three
azaleas
were
so
bound
that
sun
rain
Milky
ocean-
auroras
could
not
touch
one
only.

And
when
the
youngest
sister
burst
into
flame
perfect
flashing
a
trio
of
wrens
came
to
worship.

And
crows—
three—
to
mock
the
worshipping.

Then
the
expected
unraveling
skein
of
lonely
vultures
circled.

Privacy curtain

        Nurse said to draw the privacy curtain around the resident—
said, It makes the resident's world larger, do you see?

Because I couldn't see, she said, Lie down, young man,
        and pushed me lightly onto the other empty bed, and took a

step back, smiled as my neck and hips and knees lowered.
        She said, Look at you. I've already made you—I've unfolded

and spread and smoothed and tight-tucked you like layers
        of bedding, and have turned you down neatly—that is what we

assigned do, who are the assigners, too. We join you in
        the cradle holding your changing form. We learn you.

The rustling pages of the old resident's breathing subsided—
        his life-leaving sound was his only tongue and was, now, mine.

Pretend, she said, that you are small and still, and all
        who aren't the residents of your world will have to draw aside

their wonder-horror with their fists in order to look at you, tiny as
        a flax seed fallen there from some nonresident's chin or apron,

as quiet and as inhumanly venerable and vulnerably
        human as anything you've ever seen from a distance higher

than any distance you have known or dreamed.
        The curving sounds of the curtain rings travel through

and through you and the residents to whom we are
        assigned. Our opening faces are the stunned

curved faces of lilies the full sun has moved beyond
        the furthest possibilities of last-blooming.

What are you doing, love? This isn't the time for you
        to nap—get up, Nurse said. Come outside now. We'll have

a smoke in the lot, throw our butts at the new electrified fence
        to test the limits of the charged fields of darkness.

And I'll button my blouse so you'll look at my old
        face. Gaze as long as you wish. I assign you this.

Mr. Shadowgee's blues

This song is called the broken-axle blues because
of that ca-THUMP-ca-THUMP-ca-THUMP, a sorry sound,
a shrugging, shaking, pause-grind-pause-grind-grind-pause
you dance by shifting stance, dropping your shoulders down.

You press your tongue-tip where you find a mouth harp draw
and seal your lips tight onto a kiss-blow-kiss-blow.

Your lover's somewhere tavern-touring, rubbing raw
and rubbing raw the sins she thinks you ought to know.

You start to sing but stomp instead and darkly moan
like moaning could bring you or her or your song home.

They call that ugly stomp-cry-stomp the miner's moan—
your caged harp quits, heart quiets, too, and mines a hymn
it never heard before, broken good, broken down,
no turnaround no matter how far in you've gone.

Solstice, December 21, 2019

                                        In order to winter
              his narrow beds
                      he spread hay upon
              them and for reasons he
                              could not comprehend
                                      he carefully leveled
everything out
                          and stamped his feet over
                                  that layer and imagined
                      another he would spread
                                  sparsely would
              stamp down in a restrained
                                          but passionate tango.

                          He imagined snow
in so light a veiling
                      that the patterned chaos of stalks
              and stems would become
                          translucently evident.
                                      And he summoned an ice
                              storm making each bed
                      a window not quite
              but almost clear and each one
                                  reflecting freighted moving

              clouds. And he thought that
clouds inside the clouds would
                  be welcomed so he added some. And
                                      from the cloud-bearing
              clouds bloomed orchestral white-faced hornets
                      their stinging song
                                  recollecting for him the roadside
advertisement "Let Us Solve Your Gutter Problem!"
              the lucrative business owned by Jean

                    the son of his boyhood
                    singing teacher Mrs. Passerat
            whom he could now see peering
out through every darkening window

                            her thick makeup
            scratched glass lenses
                    silver hair rickthatched with bobby pins
            the winged sleeves of her white blouses
                            creating an effect of armless
            wristless pale fingers touching pressing
                            chording releasing.

                    Mrs. Passerat so she herself said
            would not—no matter what—ever die—
said *The Great Teachers never do—you don't*
    yet know this do you—
                            that day will come.

Prayer in response to your fearful thoughts regarding critical race theory

May thoughts of mercy
arise only after the acts.
May the thought of peace
arise only after the truce.
May thoughts of caring
arise only after giving.

May you not retreat
from acts of love to
remote thoughts of love—
no matter the price.

May your caring come first.

May your peace be held fast.

May mercy light your face.

May you hear the pure note you sing
and from inside the holy sound
may you feel what you are finding
before you think what you have found.

Mrs. P, 1962:
A singing lesson on arpeggio and glissando

"How do you keep the music playing?
How do you make it last?
How do you keep the song from fading
Too fast?"
Johnny Mathis rendition, "How Do You Keep the Music Playing?"

Arpeggio articulates each quality
of song your body dreams and breath awakens.
Glissando honors holy subtlety.

Arpeggio marks time's firm continuity;
the way that wind sounds long-leaf pines,
arpeggio articulates each quality.

When thawing snow and beading rain shines
and needles and stems become a melting rosary,
glissando honors holy subtlety.

You'll never be the singer I dreamed I
could be. My voice, outliving mere humans,
articulated each transcendent quality.

Young bee, commit your heart and memory
to hearing from within you the divine
glissando honoring holy subtlety.

The song ahead is an immensity.
Let broken cries and cries unbreaking in.
Arpeggio articulates each quality.
Glissando honors holy subtlety.

Ore

                  Tried out my
          crutches in the river
last night late
      slick steep bank
        swift waist-high flow
              light sleet needling my
     bald spot bulls-eye
       crash-boot rocking
            forward and back like a
one-leg duck misleading
     duck troop maneuvers

        undercurrent untying my
           other ill-fitting boot
    cheap piece of shit

        slipstream lapping
           against my gut
straining my leather belt

     forgot headlamp
       forgot return route
          remembered the unwrapped
    lemon drop stuck
     in my shirt pocket

         fished it out to look
gave the elusive ore
    coated in pocket lint the
      lovingest kiss of my
         whole existence

almost dropped that one
      taste of happiness in the
              merciless drink

losing—almost—
      the treasure inside the treasure nest.

Ultima Multis

The polishing
rag folded inside a
bespoke vest I purchased
on impulse has a name
sewn on by hand:
Ultima Multis.

And when I'm shining
my mouth harps after
a solitary session of practice,
I ask the piece of flag
if she knows when,
When will this end?

All of us who breathed out
and breathed in music
now ask our songs
to ask the same question
that everyone asks:
When will this end?

When will this—
our plastic curtains drawn
around our right to contagion,
to final desperate drags
from machine lungs—
when will this end?

Ultima, weren't we citizens of a
rowdy, unbuckled band
finding then losing the
groove and tipping in new
players who'd blow us apart,
who'd knock off our crowns?

Ultima, Ultima Multis,
were we—before our
breath-crushing hatred of the
world's strange other songs—
were we beautiful in our big
first hours of shining sound?

I ask you. I ask you this,
Ultima. Ultima Multis.

—there one lies at ease

High winds
cleansed distant trees
in foreign lands. Shrouded
us in petals, then deep beneath
high mounds—
there one lies at ease.

I am not a robot.

       I have clicked on the captcha Doors,
twelve in the puzzling square houses.
       I have clicked on the unmade Beds,
three in the ten square rooms.
       I have clicked on the Moons
alone behind clouds, two
vague crescents in eighteen
convincing choices of sky.
       Clicked on occupied Rooms,
drapes open inside some;
in others, the drapes drawn.
       Clicked on one isolated
Window, one visitor
there, a child, hand waving—
I have looked for her in
other proof-of-human
options, because she knows
me or I know her—or
I believe I knew her.
       Clicked on the wall Clocks set
at twelve minutes after twelve,
their white faces all named
Regulator, none wrong
by a single minute.
       Clicked on the Rockets, five
rockets leaving launching
pads depicted from such
great distances that I
had to make a guess, and
guessed humanly, and earned

the green checkmark as proof,
but worried about the
outcomes were I to fail
the sempiternal tests.

Not a robot, not yet,
        I've clicked on the Cars, so
many kinds going and
coming, no one driving
except in one; and inside
that one vehicle, perfect though
hand-drawn, I've entered the dark
systems of tunnels lit
shaft upon shaft by the dawn.

Cardiological

Your heart, a strong heart, will
say, *"Fuck you!"* and stop—
full, final, killing stop.
*"I've had enough of this
long sleeplessness, Mack,
of never resting, not
for one long stretch of night
or one downshifting nap."*

You think that sudden death
is best for you and all
of us over and done
with you, and ready to
move on through you, past you.

And, cruel to your own heart,
you keep denying that
you hear Death say, *"Fuck you,
sweet lover, fu-uck you!"*

You think you've lived awake
since birth, why take the drugs
to slow the race that's made
your punching, punching fist
of muscle stronger through
the bouts of what you call
the day your days give you.

Romantic shit like that
insults your own heart, makes
things worse. It's like you want
to run from all the debts
you owe, the ones that grow
each year—it's cowardice—
it's worse than cowardice

to whisper, "Fuck you, Death!"
if you can't face the slow
decline life brings to us.

      My cardiologist,
      my ex, vows all of this
      prognosis is true—I
      must listen now. I must.
      She pats my heart that her
      heart has survived quite well.

      And bitterly laughing,
      she says,
I'll see you in a year—
or likely not, you fool.
You can dress or, hell, just stay
the way you are for all Death
or I or anyone
else cares—or ever will.

      I should not say, but say anyway,
      "Tell Life I kept my appointment here."

Kiln

for Chris Burnham

      I cemented together the broken
clay cup, twelve pieces except for
a missing diamond-shaped chip
halfway between the bottom and
the lip, a second opening
pouring forth half of
the fullness poured in,
half of the air breathed
down, half of the last
sunlight, half of
the snowmelt,
half of the first
perfections of starlight.

Thirty-one years ago the potter
had lived in a monastery
on an island of roots and trees
and no land—a place that I,
who sent him, had always
dreamed of going.

The trees gave no fruit and
nothing of their limbs
or bark or roots was edible
though the leaves purified the
unending rain and the
roots sweetened the taste.

The monks put their dissolving
nails and teeth and the
hair falling from their
faces and heads
and bodies into the clay slip
and they brushed the paste over
the cup's smooth skin.

They sipped more
slip, thinned it with
their spit, spat inside to
coat the cup's throat.
They swallowed the
mud in their mouths
and smiled at the thought
that they could make
more cups with their
own porous, mineral shit.

When they were brought
out of the kiln the surface
of them would not
stop sparking, would
not start cooling, would
not stop living.

       Leaving the island after
eleven years there, he chose
one cup that no monk could
remember creating. He
crushed it underfoot, the
the habit of their order, and he
brought me this gift in
a ripped black sock.

He said, "We were dying, we
were dying. But we did not
feel cold, hunger, regret.
We ate mud, drank rain, and

over time we were so
clay-soaked that we
stopped wearing clothing, we
slept standing, prayed
bowed and dripping.

"I lived inside this
cup," he said.

Together he & I
put a candle in.

We watched the
seams glowing.

We listened to the
fire singing.

Afterword

In 2021, my husband Kevin "Mc" McIlvoy declared to me and other writing friends that he was turning away from writing fiction. Having published by that point eight books of fiction, and having studied and written poems all his life, he at last felt ready to go public with his poetry. At the time of his sudden death in September 2022, over two dozen of his poems were published or forthcoming, and he'd finished two full manuscripts, titled *The River Scratch* and *What a Dancer Does*. I wanted very much to complete Mc's aspiration by bringing out a posthumous poetry collection, but as all my editing and publishing experience is in prose, I couldn't do it on my own. Imagine, then, my delight and relief when Mc's friend and early reader the poet Sebastian Matthews offered to compile a manuscript and help guide it to publication. He expertly curated selections from the two manuscripts, retaining much of Mc's original sequencing, and he added—from a folder of completed but uncollected poems— the Mrs. Passerat series, conferring thematic unity and the evocative title. *Singing Lessons* simply would not exist without Sebastian's commitment, skill, and vision. I am endlessly grateful.

I am equally grateful to Kevin Morgan Watson, editor in chief and publisher at Press 53, for honoring Mc's unique artistry by bringing this book into print. I offer a heartfelt thank you as well to Mc's long-time colleague the poet Brooks Haxton for gracefully contextualizing in his introduction this newest manifestation of Mc's writing. And, many, many thanks to Alberto Rios, Sheila Fiona Black, Patrick Donnelly, and Polly Buckingham for thoughtfully, lovingly endorsing and celebrating these poems.

Christine Hale
Asheville, North Carolina
December, 2023

Acknowledgments

Grateful acknowledgment is offered to the following publications in which these poems (or earlier versions of them) have appeared:

A Species Four Million Years in Becoming: Selections from The House Party Reading Series, "I would give, I tell you" and "Tilt-up," August 2021, Ed. Ross White, Bull City Press, NC 2021

Asheville Poetry Review, Spring 2023, "The Man Rose," "Click & drag to look around," "Radicle," "Gemels," and "Mrs. Passerat transmits the gospel, 1968"

Barzakh, 2021, "The daylight waltz"

Bluestem Magazine, December 2022, "Seating chart" and "Ore"

Duality, Spring 2023, "Oh, that."

Hearth & Coffin, March 2021, "Comparable miracles" and "Another miracle in the life of Sam Sierra"

Hole in the Head Review, No. 2, February, 2022, "Descriptions of heaven"

Humana Obscura, Spring 2021, "The fit of some thing against somethings"

LEON, February 2021, "Cairn"

New Note Poetry, Spring 2022, "A golden ratio day"

Olney, Summer 2021, "Once, walking"

Scoundrel Time, December 2022, "*Ultima Multis*"

Still: A Journal, October 2021, "Nap"

Terrain.org, November 2022, "Prayer in response to your fearful thoughts regarding critical race theory"

The American Journal of Poetry, Jan. 1, 2022, "I am not a robot"

The Common, December 2022, "Sycamore, Golden Shovel," and "Kiln"

The Night Heron Barks, Winter 2021, "Troubled guest"

The Shore, Issue 13, Spring, 2022, "Privacy curtain"

Unbroken #35, October 2022, "Prose poem by God"

Willow Springs, Vols. 86-87, Fall and Spring 2021, "At 70" and "Awake, thinking himself asleep"

Notes

Awake, thinking himself asleep (p.16)
"And he's awake who thinks himself asleep" is the last line in an untitled sonnet (written in 1818) by John Keats.

Troubled guest (p.21)
The title of this poem is from "The Holy Longing" by Johann Wolfgang von Goethe: "And as long as you haven't experienced / This: to die and so to grow, / You are only a troubled guest / On the dark earth…"

Interrupting Issa's nap (p.41)
Written from inside the sleeves of two poems by Issa (trans. Sam Hamill): "The young sparrows / return into Jizō's sleeve / for sanctuary" and "My noontime nap / disrupted by voices singing / rice-planting songs."

Seating chart (p.48)
This poem includes the alteration of a line from Samuel Taylor Coleridge's "The Rime of the Ancient Mariner": "The Devil knows how to row."

Selfie (p.69)
Date reference: January 6, 2020, Trump insurrectionists storm the U.S. Capitol, kill 5, injure 140.

Oh, that (p.71)
Date reference: December 15, 2020, record-setting "mass fatality" pandemic deaths reported.

Tribute (p.72)
Date reference: November 19, 2020, Rudy Giuliani press conference, head-leaking episode.

If it's clear where you are (p.79)
The third paragraph of this prose poem is lifted (with permission) in entirety from a FB post on December 21, 2020, the planetary conjunction, by the poet Brooks Haxton.

Stacey Abrams returns to Troup County, Georgia (p.82)
This poem makes indirect reference to a passage (pgs. 81-82) from *Our Time Is Now* by Stacey Abrams. Date reference: March 7, 2021, fifty-sixth anniversary of "Bloody Sunday," the Selma to Montgomery march for civil rights.

Once, walking (p.89)
Some of this poem's imagery is indebted to W.B. Yeats' "He Wishes for the Cloths of Heaven."
Earlier versions of the Yeats poem were entitled, "Aedh Wishes for the Cloths of Heaven."

Sycamore (p.94)
This golden shovel poem includes three lines from Tony Hoagland's poem, "Barton Springs": "there just might be time to catch up on praise" and "Oh life, how I loved your cold spring mornings" and "so I will have all the time I need." The poem references the gospel of Luke 19:1-4: "And Jesus entered and passed through Jericho. And, behold, there was a man named Zacchaeus, which was the chief among the publicans, and he was rich. And he sought to see who Jesus was; and could not for the press, because he was of little stature. And he ran before, and climbed up into a sycamore tree to see him: for he was to pass that way."

Finches (p.95)
This poem references—and freely revises—a scientific study by Wenchan Zhao, Francisco Garcia-Oscos, Daniel Dinh, Todd F. Roberts, "Inception of memories that guide vocal learning in the songbird." *Science*, 2019.

The fit of some thing against somethings (p.101)
The title is borrowed from Alan Ansen's poem, "A Fit of Something Against Something."

Mr. Shadowgee's blues (p.105)
"Shadowgee," is the name for the homemade lamp that a miner of an early era constructed from an open tobacco tin with a candle fitted inside and a wire handle fixed outside.

Ultima Multis (p.112)
The words *Ultima Multis* ("the last day for many") appear on the Ibiza cathedral clock.

—there one lies at ease (p.114)
This cinquain's title comes from a line in "Death Fugue" by Pierre Joris: "we dig a grave in the air there one lies at ease"

I am not a robot (p.115)
The word "captcha" in this poem refers to the acronym CAPTCHA: Completely Auto-mated Public Turing Test to tell Computers and Humans Apart.

Kevin McIlvoy's poems appeared in *The American Journal of Poetry*, *Asheville Poetry Review*, *Barzakh*, *The Common*, *Consequence*, *The Georgia Review*, *LEON*, *The Night Heron Barks*, *River Heron Review*, *The Shore*, *Scoundrel Time*, *Superstition Review*, *Willow Springs*, *Your Impossible Voice*, and numerous other magazines. He was the author of six novels and three collections of short fiction and prose poems, including *Is It So? Glimpses, Glyphs, & Found Novels* (WTAW Press, 2023). For twenty-seven years he was editor in chief of the literary magazine, *Puerto del Sol*. He taught in the Warren Wilson College MFA Program in Creative Writing from 1987 to 2019, and as a Regents Professor of Creative Writing in the New Mexico State University MFA Program from 1981 to 2008.

www.ingramcontent.com/pod-product-compliance
Lightning Source LLC
Chambersburg PA
CBHW021405090426
42742CB00009B/1017